My Brain's Foundation

POEMS BY

Cameron Simpson

Published by Amazon in 2021

ISBN: 979-851804-012-0

Cover Design: Stuart Simpson

Contents

POSTCODE

PAIN YOU IGNORE

MY...

A LITTLE TRUTH...
A LITTLE FANTASY: Part 1

A LITTLE TRUTH...

A LITTLE FANTASY: Part 2

A TRUE SEND OFF

POSTCODE

Trigger Warning

What you are now holding is a lethal firearm.
If you are willing to go through with it,
take off the safety.
Take note, this firearm can make you trigger happy,
if you are not easily triggered, please take your position,
there is one condition.
One rule. Don't shoot the instructor.
If you are easily triggered,
please put down the firearm and leave the shooting
range.

M16

The force is like a drum kick,
it rattles in your hand like a tambourine,
in a not yet worn hands of a teen.
The instrument is broken down into pieces,
to make a paintbrush that smudges red down the
hallways.
Leaving what you call,
art.
Then it's taken home polished and cleaned,
placed on display like a trophy on the wall.

Smoking Barrels

Soul taking, smoke leave the skin baking,
stones for the yard need making.
Clip.
Snap.
Flash.
Without a lens.
But still left shattered glass,
most likely over brass.
Now the roads can taste the copper,
flashing light, dark night, road locked off by a copper.
In the road is a river, red.
You most likely sawn and read,
off the front of a magazine.
Clips holding together the paper,
the trigger letting shells off out the clip, the magazine,
spread across the street longer than a limousine.
No evidence. No street cam. No-one to pin it on.
They made sure the pin was in. Now the target has
gone.
There was no witness in sight.
Probably if there was, they would have been in the same
sight,
would have been two homicides in one night.
The family can't get to grips that their son is gone,
all they understand is someone was holding the grip and
got a tip,
nothing to sip, they weren't tipsy because they didn't
miss.

Anyone could have been behind the mask. But the tool is
murderer.
The tool brings power. Handed to fool.
Tap tap a life gone.

Drip drip. Someone left the tap on, now the body is drained.
Someone trying to stuff bin bags down the drain.
Power in the hands of a man that ain't sane.
Bullets examine a brain.
Left splatted. Left a pattern.
On every city. Every street corner.
Felt heat like it was in a sauna.
Even in snow. There is still summer.

Environment

When the environment speaks,
our actions do what they are told,
out in the black market our soul is now sold.
I lost my faith.
We carry a cross wrapped around a firearm or a sword,
I bet that sends a shock down to Lord,
feeling like he's in an interrogation room attached to a cord.
This is how we cope.
I carry my words in my mouth weighed down from a rope.
I say the wrong word, it's a game of hangman.
They say the wrong word,
then the favour tilts in ours and the gunmen lean.
They ain't too keen on liver so they aim for the breast,
or the bullet analysis of the skull like an x-ray,
a visit from the grim reaper they say,
it's a point marked on the tally for our team.
They say television whispers to your kids,
peer pressuring them into a violent scene.
Go play outside kids,
there ain't no needles or bullet shells on the ground,
or blades and axes in bushes to be found.
If you listen carefully you can hear the click of the magazine,
it's like birds singing, then bang ain't that a beautiful sound.
Don't worry kids,
it's just an old exhaust in an alleyway behind our house.
Are you crazy?
Or just lazy?
Have you been outside in London?
A person's voice ain't on this tick list,
isn't even a choice, there ain't no option.

So, the environment speaks for them,
their actions do what they are told,
till the people wave their words around like a torch,
till the city is on fire.
The government are the best at theatre, the way they act innocent,
"we will do our best" they say, I say "liar".
The environment speaks,
our actions do what they are told.

Gang

Gang.
Guns.
Drugs.
Money makes trap stars.
All I want is a percentage of that pie chart,
really, I'm going to lie and depart.
I'm stone on the surface and rubble inside,
I had to pawn my heart,
for a sawn off.
I have no plans for buying it back,
because it's shrunk too much to fit back in place.
I take that back, I'll buy it back,
break it down into bullets,
put them in a magazine called rage.
A different postcode can make me flip a page.
I'm only fifteen,
every day I'm adding a letter to my tombstone,
I could really die at this age.
My cigarettes,
every inhale forming cancer cells in my body,
actually, becomes the least of my problems.
A fatal knife wound,
on these streets is the cure to cancer,
with graveyards looking like paradise rather than hell,
rather than a cell.
I know a kid,
that never felt the blanket of the sand hugging his toes,
the fresh sea water like voices in a food market,
crowding the air in Spain.
Every day he just sees the blocks,
sees the hood,
his mum's screaming for thirst in pain.
If another kids glass is half empty or full,
he's drinking that, not spilling a drop.

He believes he deserves it more,
even if the kid's blood is sprayed on the wall like graffiti.
Takes the blood money and invest it in a crop.
Now, he's really got money growing on trees,
he's got a bad habit though he takes the money,
a rizzler rolls it up and smokes so much he's lost the plot,
the tree so off balanced now,
it tumbles over and shatters the pot.
Now, he's got to borrow money from the devil,
if he doesn't pay on time,
the hoods turning to ash like a forest fire.
The grim posts a message on Snapchat,
he's ready for hire,
is this the last letter on the tombstone?
He gets that sawn off he's been keeping,
in an old brown rusted military box in the woods.
He's now itching for blood,
if it's taken right, he knows he'll get the money.
He makes the plan with the gang and it goes well,
but like I said, if knife wounds are fatal,
everyone wants more of the cash,
so just a little off centre, it slides through his back,
bursting open his heart, spitting blood out the exit wound,
dripping down his back.
Fifteen. He really did die at that age.
Made it on the front cover of that magazine,
didn't even need to flip the page.

Gasoline

An unsettling atmosphere filled with paranoid thoughts.
Every creak and crack, every drop of water in the sink,
was yanking my soul from my flesh,
feeling like I am losing my mind,
I think I need a shrink.
No-one speaks around here.
No-one is well spoken, only straight to the point slang.
You start asking questions,
you're automatically a snitch,
a semi-automatic that goes bang.
So, we stay sat in silence,
smoking cigarettes and marijuana,
weighing up what looks like baking powder,
and every siren flying past the flat seems louder.
I haven't felt the cool breeze against my face,
or smelt the fresh air;
I think I've lost count of the weeks.
The smell and tastes in a sickened room full of gas,
I can feel the icy water on the back of my neck,
where it falls through the ceiling, where there is a leak.
No natural light can break into the room,
every crack and gap boarded up, just blue light we
consume.
Drugs we use to stay sane,
which ironically decreases my mental health,
and leaves me in pain.
Sitting here on this dusty scrap yard of a sofa,
thinking how did I get here?
Sat with my brothers believing selling drugs was the best
idea,
all I've done is sold my freedom,
stacking blue notes that are worthless, they don't buy
freedom.
Thinking I need a miracle, or I need a bit of magic,

a one-way ticket on that express,
which is seeming too far-fetched.
Knowing I'm a product of my environment,
a thug, a hired solider, money buys bodies,
so, if not in the trap house, I'm pulling up to an address.
A deep burning scar that will stay with that family for
life,
left with PTSD.
The trigger left shells,
left their son's body, unable to identify, a mother in
distress.
Life around here is game of chess,
if I make the right move,
you might see me dressed in the finest silk,
but I'm far from blessed.
I make the wrong move and it's a different game.
The wrong word we'll be playing hangman,
police trying to remove the noose,
this environment will never improve.
We are either in a black hole of depression,
and hang ourselves, or we are hung for our aggression.
Locked in cages because we don't understand
confession, because I can't tell you no-one's description.
'No comment' already signed my life's subscription,
I didn't read the small print, the encryption.
The code on my vest for life,
'til the grim reaper pays a visit,
after it's taken with a knife.
Ironically, my DNA covered the cell,
off goes the bell,
my damaged soul straight to hell.

Cigarettes of Violence: Part 1

Sharp pains in my legs off unorthodox bricks
and daggers of stones, as I lean against a fallen wall.
A red rim,
puffs of smoke from different directions,
then ash fills the air,
an erupting volcano,
our cigarette buds fall.
An uneasy atmosphere of awkward laughter,
then after followed the nervous silence.
As I look around, I see five kids acting like five men,
who never had guidance.
A red mist covered fearless and emotionless cold blue
eyes,
'til you entered the darkness in the middle of my eyes,
to see the trembling kid inside,
which had to be shoved aside.
I see twitching hands, the wrinkles of clinching fists,
the uncontrollable tapping.
I see the same thought on everyone's faces lapping.
The slight movements I make,
the clashing of metal,
is making everyone more unsettled.
The single sliver of sweat makes its way down my pale
icy skin, under my mask.
The bitter taste on my lips from a flask.
A dark unsettling red stain on the end of my sleeve.
A bag hits the ground which felt like the earth shaking,
which was filled with garden tools, bats and blades,
for a goal I wasn't sure I could achieve.
Stomach pains,
sounds of a vicious dog,
smoke filled my inside with fog.
Time came to a stop, then it was time to leave,

back of a car, my heading spinning,
like Mars blood stains cover my arms.
There was no more hiding the fear in my eyes,
the glittering gloss of sweat, from head to toe,
I'm now my worse foe.

Put Out the Cigarettes: Part 2

It was time to leave.
Before I step on the overcrowded,
suffocating and sweaty bus,
I put out my cigarette.
We are on our way now, I had to leave her behind,
regret.
I left her at the bus stop, along with good intentions,
on this journey, I don't need an intervention.
I know my place in hell has already been reserved.
Over every speed bump, the tool in my pocket,
makes an explosion of sound.
Eyes target on me like heat seeking missiles,
their thoughts and smug faces,
trying to bury me in the ground.
Feeling like a little kid again, kicking and screaming,
throwing uncomfortable behaviour at stranger,
making them feel awkward,
then in a gust of relief they turn away.
I turn to say,
my answer is in my sight,
I turn an unhealthy ghostly colour,
as I know deep down my actions are far from right.
We step off.
Into an unknown hostile environment,
a warning sign written out as a postcode,
then I hear the whispers of shells, rolling on the road.
I grip my pocket a little bit tighter.
Then we see it,
I call it that because if I give it a name, I give it purpose,
but money speaks over purpose.
My legs start to cut through the barriers of air,
I lunge forward, slipping through alleyways,
diving over a gate, whilst tugging my mask down,

before a camera confirms my fate.
I throw my hand out of my pocket,
then swing my arm with all my force,
nearly detaching my bones.
Feathers blind my vision, tinted a dark red.
I launch my body into a one eighty,
skinning my cheek on barbed wire,
a subtle tear glides down my head.
Retracing our steps back,
I hear the howls of blood thirsty animals,
following our tracks.
The snaps of magazines and chambers pulling back.
I fly through the air like a rag doll, hitting the bus floor,
and like that we are gone into the distance.
Shaking viciously, trembling, teeth grinding,
my body and my brain need assistance.
Back home trying to light a cigarette,
more burns on my fingers than smoke in my lungs.
Need something with a bit more of a punch,
I fill my lungs with marijuana.
A car pulls up...

Quit Smoking: Part 3

A car pulls up.
Like a tornado, I'm swept off my feet,
plunged straight into the back,
my head spinning like Mars, blood stains cover my arms.
There was no more hiding the fear in my eyes,
the glittering gloss of sweat covered me head to toe,
I'm now my worst foe.
My clothes reek,
turning my stomach into a washing machine,
on a long spin.
Battle scars written all over my face,
branded on me like a sin.
My stomach gives up and is now free falling.
The unknown figure glances back at me, with such a
grin,
meaning my stomach wasn't calming anytime soon,
I could imagine it escaping my body,
sprinting away like an over-dramatic cartoon.
My chest starts to cave and crumble in on itself,
my throat clogs up and my breathing becomes manual.

The brother.
He is still wearing his younger brother's blood,
still fresh.
I can almost taste the copper in the air,
an over-powering meaty flesh.
I twitch my foot, it comes into contact with soft rocks,
wet soil, recently pulled from the earth,
then I feel the shovel.
My fear grows like an infection,
my eyes start to boil.
The brakes let out a loud piercing sound,
the hand brake slammed on,
and I'm flipped out the car.

A hole in the ground is presented to me,
the mountain high soil shadows over me,
like I'm already underneath.
A frozen chunk of metal is engraved in my forehead,
a flash, followed with a chunk of lead,
that examines my brain.
A red rim.
A puff of smoke from one direction,
the smoke fills my skull likes it's made a connection.
My corpse attaches itself to earth.

PAIN YOU IGNORE
Warning: Emotional content

Skip if easily offended

MH

It's crazy how every thought feels like I fought a battle,
trying to arrange the good and bad like cattle.
It's crazy how every thought taught me something new,
pain in my veins,
knowing I'm far from sane.
A screw loose, an extra for my coffin.
The norm I've never felt,
the tears,
the fears.
A loveless heart.
Cold.
That came to melt.

Friendships that taught me,
that even the strongest boat will become a shipwreck.
A sick head, which is easily bred on the streets,
covered in shells from a Tec.
A sick mind, where violence was the norm.
Violence is a part of me, a partner, an alliance.
When the storm ends,
how do you come to a stop?
The body torn down like crops.
Hands clean,
but what was seen,
will carry stains of blood through the mind.

A heart stitched together over and over,
'til there was no more string.
Pain an uncomfortable ring.

Never to leave, and peace to never receive.
Anger that holds together the bones,
anger to change peoples' tones.
A jealous rage, to want an imaginary throne.

Problems passed down through DNA,
through the environment.
Things you can't learn in books for an assignment.
Rows of eyes, which with a look,
can crack the most stable of people.
Not pity but disgust.
Like I'm a hazard.

A temper that is unleashed like a beast with no warning.
A sick mind filled with anger, sadness and jealously.
I feel that.
I feel no meaning.
Anger that I brought into this world with no warning.
A society, that only knows destruction,
profit from production.
But no help. Only more pain with a smile,
an evil and cruel smile for an induction.
Pushed aside,
brushed away by my own thoughts,
like sand by the tide.
Hushed.
To suffer in silence.
Dirt on my coffin. Now there is...
Silence!

Hater

Someone who is too lazy to find the good intentions, and who fails to put the letters of their heart in the right order.

Earth

I take its letters, each one a part of the environment
that influenced the roots, which grew to make me into
the person I am today, its new arrangement of letters
formed my heart.
The purest form of art.

American Psycho

by Mary Harron and Guinevere Turner
Based on the novel by Bret Easton Ellis

Bateman:
You'll notice that my friends  look and behave in
a remarkably similar fashion

I'm

asking dumb, obvious questions about how to
dress.

Investment

You could call my happiness an investment.
I need to know how much of my heart you will cost me.
Will the risk be worth my percentage I'll be taking?
Or are you out to scam me?

I am a Soldier

I wasn't around in 1913.
I wasn't around in 1939.
I've never been to Iraq.
I've never been to Afghanistan.
But I have been to war.
I have got my hands filthy and stained on tour.
I have felt the stomach-turning feeling,
of blood washing off my arms and glossing the sink,
a diluted red, almost pink.
I have felt my family's blood,
get stuck under my nails like dried mud.
I have seen a pin float to the ground like a feather,
the click just before the grenade demolishes my home.
I have seen what war does to someone.
Not just anyone.
My family.

I've spent many frozen hours in the hospital as they
recover.
I've felt the clog,
the over-flowing of tears which are constantly pushed
back,
feeling like they're going to explode out the back of your
head,
but to the nurse they're just another.
They're just paperwork.

I have seen the layers of scars, one on top of the other,
each opened and closed, the meat exposed to the air.
What a bullet does,
when it travels two thousand six hundred feet per
second,
when it hits the flesh and causes more than a little tear.
Even when you do your best to prepare,

and wear that vest over your chest,
to cover your heart.

No.
No.
No.

No, I'm not actually talking about guns and bullets,
or people killing each other over oil.
I'm talking about mental health.
I'm talking about mothers losing their kids over a war,
which they are battling every day,
which is taking place in their head,
until they get killed in the line of duty.
Then they have to bury them under six feet of soil.

I've seen what damage a mirror does,
it's a machete gutting their confidence till it's
unrecognisable.

Their eyes are meant to be their brother in arms,
but they can't tell the difference between friendly and
the enemy,
they are unreliable.

I've seen friends trying their best to pick them up with
words,
but to them, words are like land mines, they stay clear
of them.

I've seen the walls behind their eyes that they hide
behind,
from the frightening world. The walls are a bullet proof
vest,
they won't let no-one get too close to their chest.

I've had the two-am calls where they are trying to say goodbye,
which felt like a jet that flew past, dropping bombs,
leaving the most painful ringing in my ears,
leaving me falling to the ground,
with my face painted camouflage, but with tears.

I've been to war.
I've seen friends go to war.
I've seen family go to war.
The war never ends.
Never ends
Never.
Ends.

Bruised Heart

Dear...
I write, then take the paper outside, take out a cigarette and a lighter,
torch the end of the tobacco stick, then the paper, watch as it becomes brighter,
then fades away in the wind. Then I take my pen and start again,
repeat and start again,
each time, drifting further away from a goodbye.
The door handle starts to creak, before the door slams open,
Mum asks, "are you okay?
you ok?"
I try to relax myself as I say "I'm fine",
I lie.
My tie,
a paint brush dabbing on my neck, mixing purple and green.
Calm words blind her sight, there is no need to be alarmed,
even when the fire alarms are kicking and screaming,
in your face it can't be seen.
A smile, the most effective magic trick in the book.
A magician never reveals his secrets, they don't want you to look too carefully.
I walk up the stairs to the top floor,
enter my home, bolt the locks on my door.
Last time I was here there was a flood,
I can still see the damp in spots.
I check if Joy has left any voicemails, but zero missed calls,
she had once loved...
ME.
But I cheated on her with depression.

At the time, I felt we had lost the connection,
she was right to leave.
I knew she was never coming back,
because on the tiny dark oak coffee table she had left
her key.
I felt terrible because I treated her like a caged bird,
but now she is set free,
not locked in here with the ghosts that are stuck to my
back,
like a bad rash, that only gets worse the more I scratch.
Sometimes they like to play games,
they take a thought of mine and stretch it to the point
before it snaps,
then play a game of catch.
They call the game over thinking,
They play it until my body feels exhausted, that I start
sinking.
Lying in my bed, looking at the clock,
watching the hands race each other, lapping the track.
The sun starts to do its morning stretch, before my lights
flicker and go black.
Twenty minutes later I'm going to school, sitting in class,
but starting to feel like a TV because I'm always on catch
up.
My brain's still at home, playing piggy in the middle,
they now know how to play me like a fiddle.
Through my eyes I'm watching the beautiful world,
but I only see it through a stain on the window.
I'm interrupted by the ghost voices in my ears,
telling me to distance myself from everyone,
because they can hear the whispers, that the class think
I'm a weirdo,
to the point my feet start to turn away now from school.
To bunk it, to hang with mates outside of school.
Anger, anxiety and depression.
We sit in the woods, smoking weed but then they always
leave,

I'm starting to think they ain't really into it, well that's my impression,
the rest of the time they treat me like an obsession.
I've got to the point where I'm not the biggest fan of sleepovers,
as I reach a point where I need my own time,
but they constantly need attention.
Always making me watch films that make my muscles grow tighter,
building too much tension that I start to cry.
Telling me I have to be quiet, keep myself to myself,
my friends' parents just think I'm shy.
My mum has told me now,
that she doesn't want me hanging out with them anymore,
they ain't good for me.
I try to go my separate way and depart.
The next time I have a pen,
it's made of my heart, writing goodbye,
on a piece of paper signing it with a tear.
Dear...
I write, then take the paper outside.

Drive

I don't need the key to solve my problems, it's in the
ignition.
The waves of music that demolish at the base of the cliff,
keeping my problems at their peak.
The window cracked open,
a gust of relief smacking me in the face,
making me realise I'm actually strong, and not as weak.
The exhaust spitting out the smoke,
which is the steam from my brain, which is boiling
away.
But in this car,
the line of riot,
shields guarding the stunning view is my biggest
problem.
Our out of tune voices, filled with purest joy,
bounce from side to side, within the car.

We drive on and on,
turning off 'Troubles Road',
almost like we jumped off,
as if we were the toad.

Confidence

I followed the instructions, to build my confidence up like
Lego bricks,
but there is always a piece missing.

Like a cat purring, until your hand passes over the wrong
spot,
a cut that hadn't healed properly, now it's hissing.

I finally finish my tower, a shadowing insult in the form
of a finger,
pushes the wrong brick.
My tower comes down like Jenga.

Switch

My insides have become a furnace,
using the blood which flows through my veins as its fuel,
until it catches fire and spreads rapidly through my
entire body.
I call it anger.
Ever since being a kid, I have worn it like a baggy
hoodie.
Printing my forehead against the wall,
not realising I'd asked the printer for a hundred plus
copies.

Switch.

I'm light years away on my own planet,
as I sync like Bluetooth with my video games.

Switch.

My hands built like a hammer,
as I smash the controller into fragments,
I steal its purpose away from it like a thief.

Switch.

My eyes start to gloss,
as a kid I feel like I'm holding a crime scene in the palm
of my hands.

Every year that goes by,
like a passing car on the motorway,
you would think I'd have grown out of the hoodie by
now,
but until this day, it's the only clean clothes that fit me.
People talk about the blue moon,

but I have only seen the sky blue,
when my eyes are covered with tears.
After the chaos I had brought down around me like a tsunami,
through my lens the sky is a red mist.

Throughout my life, my anger is like having 'test me' printed on my face,
kids seem to love putting me through an exam.
As usual I'd try to skip and hide out back to roll up a gram.
As usual a teacher would catch me and force me to do my practical.
As usual the other kids would end up with the highest marks.
It was like a toddler playing with a light switch.
On.
Off.
On.
Off.
Until the wire overheated, then sparked,
sometimes causing a fire,
or just a little bit of light, until it would eventually fizzle out.
But if someone interacted with the switch again,
if it's straight after the recent spark,
it would end in a total black out.

My anger is like that friend your parents always tell you ain't good for you,
you argue with them for hours believing you are on the winning side,
and that you will prove them wrong.
They are right...
that friend will always pull you to the left,
until one day that means they have left.

Leaving the paperwork in the form of trouble slammed
onto your desk,
for you to sift through and reorganise.
A horrendous smelling rugby kit,
that you still wear...
head tilted to the ground, ashamed.
A toxic ex that you always crawl back to,
on your hands and knees like a dog, with them holding
the leash.
Head tilted to the ground, ashamed.
A loose baby tooth that you try to pull out,
but brings you more pain than it's worth, so you leave it
in place.
A briefcase handcuffed to your hand,
turns out I lost the key.

My anger is my only tattoo.
I'm not happy with it,
but I don't have the funds to get it lasered off,
and even if I did, the scar would always stay.

Before Social Media

Before my body was judged like *X Factor,*
a stage viewed by thousands of people through glass.
Before I felt like my mirror had a foul mouth.
Before a comment got posted directly to my brain,
driving me insane until it became an uncontrollable pain.
Before likes were treated like a video game level.
Before my friends became the final boss,
I had been training for months,
and I was going to beat them whatever it cost.
Before I cared.
Before peoples' thoughts became a thriller and I was
truly scared.
Before.
Before I lost my true self.
Before my honest thoughts went missing,
and I had to send out a search party,
but they never found the body.
Before I could be shaped like clay.
Before I was told what was cool to say.
Before I planned my post,
as if it was a heist searching for the flaws,
making sure I couldn't be caught, being nothing but a
trend.
Before I spent half of my day debating whether to click
send.
Before group chats were the new team death match.
Before.
Before I signed up to be an actor,
trying to be the lead role in the new drama.
Before I really felt the horses kick, right on the jaw from
karma.
Before girls held the launch codes to destroying your life.
Before comments cut deeper than a knife.
Before social media...

I was happy.
Truly happy.

Falling

I'm smoking on this herb, playing operations with my
brain,
trying to put the parts back in place, feeling like I'm
falling,
about to crack my head on this curb.
My thoughts telling me that my destiny is already
chiseled in the stone,
it's set to fail, so I'm finding it hard to feel merry,
which is ironic as my best friend is Merry,
but I call her Jane.
She's the only one making this sinister, never-ending
maze,
come to an end, so I can start seeing a glimpse of sane.
Starting to feel like a clown looking in a shattered mirror,
teaching myself to smile,
but this never-ending pile of messed up thoughts,
playing like a season of Black Mirror.
I open my desk, take the razor,
the red tears add a layer to my face,
trying to draw a smile on this dead stare looking back at
me,
face to face.
Like a cowboy, in a stand-off with myself.
I've truly never known myself.

Trust

My experience was like a lit match,
you can only hold on to it for so long until you get burnt.
It was very similar to money, it had to be earned.
Something that was so complicated, it was a puzzle that had to be learnt.
Running around a maze trying to find someone I could trust,
disclosing my classified information, only to find out they were a spy.
tricking, lying, deceiving me whilst looking me in the eye.
A friendship was novel, fictional and metaphorically stabbing me in the back,
literally stabbing me in arm,
pulling apart the meat shattering the elbow in a vicious attack.
A steel bridge, the paths, sprinting down them into a blur.
The masks, my friends' underneath,
my enemy crowded around me, suffocating me.
I shout the truth out, but it's overpowered by the whispers,
the lies about me.
Trust.
I just don't understand, it's made me build walls I now cower behind.
My common-sense burns to ash, my sight that once saw clearly, I'm now blind.
How foolish I could be handing it out like a freebie,
just to be thrown away like a frisbee which doesn't come back to me.
Caught in the howling wind it glides away, only to shatter into fragments.

I try so hard to pick up the pieces, but how do you pick
up dust,
when it falls though the gaps in my fingers?
That's what's left of my trust.
Like an ancient antique it just can't be replaced,
I try to make a replica, but this one is not from my
heart, not built from the same place.
Never again will I hand it out like flyers, just be torn to
pieces by liars.
Trust.
They say it's a must.
The fuel to keep a relationship running, but I feel like I'm
now gasping for air,
my lungs ache, my shins burn like a flare.
I know I'm not being fair and not everyone is the same,
but I refuse to flip the coin, because if I lose again there
is only me to blame.
Trust.

Mirror

A reflection outlining all your faults.
Trying to hide the disappointment,
pushing it down somewhere you don't go often,
your hidden vault.
Filled with the most classified thoughts.
A reflection, an illusion you see.
A reflection of you in the shape of a lie.
A reflection that spills depression down you freshly
cleaned white dress,
a stain that won't come out in a single wash.

Body dysmorphic disorder.

Self-medicating

I take my money that has lost its worth, with the idea of
buying anything other than painkillers.
The tablets come in the shape of a bottle with a red cap.
I pop it to the back of my throat, acting like it's a bottle
of bleach,
to burn away this illness that has clung to me like a
leech.
A reminder it only kills 99.9% of bacteria,
that 0.1% still hovers in the back of my brain.
Once in a while it will pass through my thoughts like a
train,
coming to a stop at overthinking station.
In the end, me and alcohol would sit on the bench at the
platform, going over old conversations.

The Cat Scratched Me

The teacher asked me, "what happened to your arm?"
my voice responds before my brain can process the
question,
I tell her, "The cat scratched me".
I start overthinking, in the frozen moment of
awkwardness I'm trapped in.
Did I leave the claws on my desk?
Did my dad see the cat I've been hiding in my room?
Is the cat out of the bag?
The thin razors that are covered in my DNA that make
up its feet.
Realising I am thinking out loud, my head spinning like
this seat.
She says "okay", then shrugs the concern from her
shoulders.
I think that's how easy, a blanket made out of lies
covers a serious problem.

MY...

My Great Grandad

My Great Grandad.
He was born on 2nd May 1925,
or 1923 if the Admiral asks.
In 2018, we stood on the dock with our emotions in our hands,
and like the motion of the waves our hands form as he boarded his ship.
As I watched through a camera with raindrops covering the lens,
his smile worked as a window wiper flicking them off,
no longer a waterfall, more like a broken tap with a drip.
The sky covered in his model planes, as his ship started to leave.

My Great Grandad was almost a silent man,
but his actions sang a thousand more words than a singer on tour.
His actions showed more love, than a "love you" rolling off the tongue,
giving his whole arm and a leg, instead of just a hand to help anyone.
Everyone.
Sometimes, I wonder if Roald Dahl had taken ideas from my Great Grandad for *Charlie and the Chocolate Factory.*
As soon as a foot was placed in his living room,
to a kid it was a live action of the factory,
more chocolate than you can imagine.
My treasured memories of him are like an Aston Martin DBR1,
only a few will share the experience of driving one,
which makes my memories feel richer.

Stood on the dock with family I had never met,
some I had not seen in years,

he would have wanted his family to come back together.
I know my Great Grandad loved to mend and repair things,
so, he did one last thing before he sailed away,
he brought me and my dad together again,
to stop the past sticking to us like a shadow and sending it astray.
An engine that had slowly rusted over the years and wouldn't start anymore,
he got it polished and running once again.
And like that, wearing his perfectly ironed Navy uniform,
he sailed off over the horizon.

Thank you, Great Grandad.

My Grandma's Famous Fruit Cake

My birthday.
Christmas.
My favourite.

All the ingredients of happy memories baked together,
take a rolling pin to flatten this slice of cake,
an hourglass of a smile on my face.
With every mouth full, my childhood goofy smile grows
wider,
using my eye as a divider.
But I always cut jagged, just for the little extra crumb,
of time travelling back to a simpler time.

"Just a little more to the left, perfect",
half a cake later.

It's not everyone's cup of tea,
but grab yourself a slice and sit around the table for a
gossip,
"Actually, I'll take two sugars with that, thanks".

A cake full of stories,
to be baked and remade,
over the family's future generations.

My Favourite Poem

My favourite poem is you.
Sometimes our rhyming, our flow is not smooth,
sometimes there's a ripple in our river or a dam in our way.
You're my wisdom tooth,
sometimes we cause each other pain, but there is only one of you.
My favourite poem is you.
I can write our beginning and introduce our middle,
my hand starts to feel frail and starts to sail off into the distance,
because I can't bring myself to write our ending,
I would rather keep guessing it like a riddle.
My favourite poem is you.
Short and meaningful,
my pen doesn't need to add or support you by yourself, you're beautiful.
But you hide in your bland cocoon.
I want to help you, let the colours out which are hiding your butterfly.
You're amazing, this smack on pie face which can't be hidden, my smile doesn't lie.
My favourite poem is you.
I want to show you off like a spoken word,
at the same time, I want to keep you as a draft on my desk,
because I want to keep you to myself sometimes,
forgetting your feelings and just choosing without knowing, which you prefer.
My favourite poem is you.
An idea perfect on paper, but turning out to be much more than I ever dreamt,
a fantasy it seemed.
My favourite poem is you.

I'm not much of a love poet,
but if I were to choose one, it would more than 100% be
you.

My Umbrella

My umbrella,

the protection in the storm.

My umbrella,

shaking off the rain drops,
the tears on my top.
The black skies, the clouds in my head,
being ripped apart like bread.

My umbrella,

covering the skies,
like the clouds had fled.
Some days when I feel like I'm barely holding on,
you teach me to handle,
any situation.
Pulling me in the wind from a bad temptation,
the warmth inside me going cold, like water on a lit
candle.
But you've got it covered and then I rediscovered,
my smile,
which has been lost for a while.

My umbrella,

my safety in the storm,
the gusting, threading bad cold,
thoughts you keep warm.
Swarms of happiness,
reform this cold heart.

My umbrella,

I wish to never be far apart.

My Blood is Magnetic

When you think of something which is magnetic,
you probably assume mineral magnetite or some sort of
metal.

But, through the experiment called life, I've found blood
to be the most magnetic material,
it always seems to pull the same group of people
together in times of need.
Also, pushing the same group of people an incredible
distance apart.
It is all controlled by the heart.

A LITTLE TRUTH...
A LITTLE FANTASY
PART 1

Hands

I was once told by a man my strongest weapon wasn't to raise my arm,
but to have an open palm.
To bruise and scar will heal and form rage,
to shake hands, make peace find common ground,
there is no need for drama on this stage.
A holy man, he was a man of peace, who based his morals by a single page,
to wish to never see a fellow man, turn to felon, locked up in a cage.
His hands stuck together as if they were taped,
always raised to the sky to pray, a simple man, not many words to say.
When he spoke, the most stained hands gave respect,
as if offerings could be washed away.
Men who would stab each other in the back, brothers they would betray,
came to hold hands when the man showed them a better way.
So, why?
A simple man, a giving man, offering a hand to anyone.
So, why?
Why now is everyone,
stood around his grave, my heart lost in a terrifying, cold, damp cave.
For a pound, from a hand came an awful sound,
a sound that buried the shards of glass,
which were his family's hearts with him in the ground.
How much was that pound really worth?
Was it really as much as another heart of gold, added back to the earth?
I was once told by a man my strongest weapon wasn't to raise my arm,
but to have an open palm.

Not to seek the revenge,
I so desperately think that will repair those cogs that
have rusted and cracked inside of me.
To show that peace is the best way to honour a man,
who could close his eyes and turn away from violence.
The world needs non-violence.
The world needs a man, a woman, a group, a
community, a country,
to show that hands don't need to be used as weapons.
Hands that create arms that burn the world adding fuel
to fire.
The world running on a worn-down tyre.
I was once told by a man to not raise my arm,
but to show them my open palm.
They will cut through its meat and break it bones,
but my actions will crack their victory like stones.

Guidance

They say you can plan your life and write down the
directions of your route,
but I would always make spelling mistakes.
Where is the satisfaction if you already know the
illustration you drew for yourself?
In front of your own eyes, none of the hard work or the
aches, blood, sweat and tears.
Stuck in the mud, your life you had to bet and the fears.
Your life can't be directed with instructions,
your life is to take the rubble of your failures and
construct your success.
Carve your journey for those to see, but only give them
the dust as guidance.

Someone to You

A Song by Banners

I don't 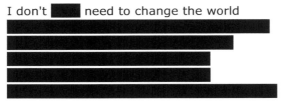 need to change the world

I just wanna be somebody to someone.

Engine

My heart works like an engine.
It needs the oil to run smoothly, an engineer to give it attention.
Without your oil, my parts will grind and seize.
My engine will be ruined.

Whisper to the Wind

I pour my heart into a cup and splash it into the clouds.

They cover the fields in crowds,
like a festival.

Just to strum my heart strings to you,
have the wind to whisper to you,
please come back.

I'll use the sun like a flashlight,
to burn through the darkness,
to open your eyes to the sight of track.
The path back home.

Love at My Door

Love.
Doesn't tell you a time.
Doesn't tell you a place.
Doesn't tell you when.
Love just knocks on your door,
whether you are dressed for the party or not.
Love can make you shy, even embarrassed at times,
spilling that drink down your favourite shirt.
But she can be the one holding the damp cloth even in
the limelight.
Love is the one cracking its way through the case of your
cocoon,
letting the butterflies fly free in the air.
The wild laughter that was chained up in a zoo,
love has shattered the links and let it back out to be
joined by its pair.
Sometimes love is an imposter, a fake,
only performed to take,
and Joy the doctor couldn't stitch up the cuts without
leaving scars.
Real love will tend to the wounds,
they will become a distance memory,
You and love will make a full documentary.

You Made

Love is a liar,
happiness is now unfaithful.
Faith has become distant, I'm pretty sure he blocked my
number or ignores my calls.
Joy figured out time travel and went back to the
medieval times to hide behind castle walls.
Kindness has become beyond the definition of laziness.
Pain is the only friend that has stuck by my side.
Pride sends postcodes occasionally.
They always say your school friends are not forever,
you will make new friends.
Taking selfies with anxiety, but never post them.
Lately, I've been in groups chats will all my new friends,
we called the group mental health,
we just talk about ourselves.

You Never Did Call

I sat forever waiting to answer.
In the end I tried.
I typed in your number and it began to ring.
Declined...
Declined...
Declined began to sing.
In the hook of the song.
I got my answer.

Graveyard

Thick piles of snow as far as the eye could see,
blurring into the distance like the sea.
Skin going purple, polished with soil,
it was so cold, even meat would not spoil.
Once a glooming forest,
now mountains high with firewood,
we were trying to get warm, for as long as we could.
Thor's hammer striking through the sky,
lashing down into the graveyard.
Blacksmiths' hammers crashing, forming the finest
swords,
with sparks, as the rest of us blood thirsty like sharks,
we stand guard.
Vicious as wild dogs, as we bark,
the gods watch over us like a lark.
Atmosphere filled with death.
The vultures and valkyries stalk the ground,
striking of axes against shields shake the valley, as if
death was a sound.
"Charge!"
Thousands, beyond thousands of boots pull the land
apart,
an ocean sky turns black, as the arrows block out the
sun,
swords strike through flesh, guts and chop off body
parts.
Splinters of wood fly through the air.
an arrow takes with it my ear, which went straight into
the eye of my peer.
Matt red drips down my face like tears,
my eyes stained red,
I know now I will fight 'til I'm dead.
My body is no longer attached to my head, mark what I
have said.

I dig my sword through the bones and tender raw flesh,
and start tearing it off, as if I have claws like bear.
I use my bare hands to crush their skulls like Thor's
hammer would,
their eyes roll away in the mud.
An axe shoots out the clouds bringing a shower of blood,
my neck starts to burn...
The world starts to scatter and blur, the ground becomes
closer.
Pitch black...
A streak of light, not yellow,
but a glossy gold in the corner of my eye, as if through a
crack.
My whole-body stone cold.
I start to mould to the stomping boots,
one with the ground like roots.
Pulled apart like pork, stretched and scattered
throughout the battlefield,
my corpse now used as a shield.
Still at war, even after death. Now watched by the gods.
A glorious death.
Valhalla awaits.

G.O.D.S.

Vikings.
Spartans.
Knights.
Samurais.
Gods.
May a valley stand tall like a giant to protect the promise
land of a warrior.
May a valley be a promise of death to a warrior.
May a valley, the snow globe ready to be shook into
chaos, of blood and screams.
Blood thicker than water still flows smoothly like the
stream.
A valley is a boxing ring, two warriors glaring at each
other,
trying to reach out and grab each other's souls.
The audience.
The crowd.
The gods.
A warrior will sever their death like a spectacular meal,
just to make their gods proud.
A man, a woman, a gravestone, gripped tightly in their
hands,
ready to offer it to a man, a woman, on the other side of
the valley.
An express ticket; a one way to ticket to their gods.
A cross.
An oath ring.
A shield.
A symbol worn as armour over their soul, so it is ready
for their afterlife.
Eyes stapled open, fearless of the slow motion, of the
movement of the knife.
Their hands now a bucket, catching the leak of liquid
oozing out,

each drop forming a step to their god.
A warrior's purpose is death.
Death's purpose is the afterlife.
Afterlife's purpose is to bring you to your maker.
You are the perfectly golden-brown bread fresh out of the oven,
ready to be sliced open by your baker.
The actions already in motion.
A warrior-built brick by brick of pride, but no cement of emotion.
Death.
Death.
Death.
Offered to many different gods and goddesses.

Beauty of the Mountain

The peak.
A glossy, sparkling blanket which hugs the alpha of the
sky,
tearing through the gentle smoke hovering by.
Pass the blanket, is the scars and the wounds that fall
deep into darkness,
only the moon's gentle beam of light, can see its
starkness.
The glooming, endless wonders dragging all creatures in.
An untouched surface by man.
No footprint but paws, the hunting ground with no laws.
A silence, beauty fills the air, then suddenly shattered
like glass,
a howl filled the sky like gas.
A daunting height which shadows the sight of many
valleys,
even the most fearless creatures turn away in fright.
The gods would never ignite a war, because it will deliver
them a serious smite.
The coronal of the land,
the general of heights.
A general respect from man and gods of the beauty and
terror of the mountain.
That stands so unfazed.
A slight smirk you can catch.
A giant that would gobble up Britain.

Beautiful Star

Many would see an endless black hole that swallows
planets and spits out fear,
I see the beauty.
The endless dreams gliding through the milky way,
pulling me near.
Many wouldn't give a second glance of her mysterious
wonderful appearance,
I would grab that chance with both hands to unravel her
secrets,
because I am completely mystified by her appearance.
Many couldn't take that one step for man,
I'm willing to crawl on all fours for my dream.
Sat here, on this solid still ground, my mind,
my eyes, sailing through the countless, endless wishing
stars.
One for every spirit to be remembered,
every person with something deep down inside them,
a void of gloominess to be filled with joyfulness.
She will provide not matter, where on this frozen or
scorching spinning planet, she is by your side,
when the chain of leeching thoughts are causing you
pain.
Tilt your head back, she will let out your inner joy of
adventures of being a child,
let your happiness run wild.

A LITTLE TRUTH...
A LITTLE FANTASY

PART 2

Hangman

Words.
Can be a lethal injection that sometimes you don't know
you are poking in,
which stays under your skin for such a long time,
and some words you curse them like a sin.
Which brings me to when I was a kid,
I was obsessed with spies, ninjas and hitmen; so much it
was my dream to be one.
As a kid,
can you image telling an adult you want to be hitman?
You'd get hung for saying it,
even as a joke.
Some words are like burying your face in food,
you will get to a point where you will choke.
They say everyone has an opinion and to shout them
out,
until you light the fire, then they tell you to put it out.
In the end people hate the truth,
if you say the wrong word, they want to play hangman.
They become a hitman.
They say what they want, even if it makes you bleed,
but they can't stand to hear what you want even if you
plead.
They are not interested in what you need.
Words are bought,
only the rich own the best of them,
and we are only allowed them in our thoughts.

System Failure: One in Seven Billion

I'm different.
I'm different.
You're different.
Copied and pasted.
We are actually the same,
you can scream and shout, maybe forge it in stone and claim,
but in the end, we are the same.
Zeros and ones, you're one or the other.
You're chasing the mysteries of the galaxy and earth like a scout,
or online bragging and like blood in your veins chasing clout.
You're putting fear in others, a dark cobble of a heart, a villain or a fearless giving hero.
One or zero.
You're zoned in, a determined gamer,
you have people calling you a nerd or someone who thinks you are cool, a claimer.
Someone suffering from mental health, trapped in a chamber or mentally stable and know yourself,
sat at the table counting your wealth or sat crumbling like a stone wall,
out in the wild a shadow to civilians, passing by like you're in stealth.
One or zero.
Passionate in the art of music, a lover or following the herd,
for the next trend, more in love with the drugs on the cover.
Needles and powder or lighting up the herb, taking off like a rocket,

medication from the pharmacy, everyone's got drugs in their pocket.
A man of arms or peace, bending their legs at their knees, palms open.
One or zero.
We as people, are always split down the middle,
a believer in the unknown, a god, different gods, but still a believer,
or fascinated by the universe that only gives you a riddle.
A system, one and zeros we are in a computer.
You claim you're different,
everyone says they are different.
One in seven billion.

Marijuana

Weed. He called it his Hannibal Lecter.
Weed. He called it his Jack Napier.
Weed. He called it his Patrick Bateman.
A psychopath that he watched with both of his eyes,
butcher his oldest friend whose name was anxiety.
He watched him be decapitated.
Ironically, who was always in his head,
a psychopath that murdered his girlfriend, her name was depression.
He watched him pull her apart,
like pulling the lining from clothes thread by thread.
He watched him take his brother whose nickname was PTSD,
drowned him in a river of relief and left him there to float.
He watched him shatter his uncle's bones,
made of glass like a mirror, his nickname was BDD.
Weed. They call it someone's Batman.
Weed. They call it someone's Ironman.
Weed. They call it's someone's Superman.
When someone has had to go to war against their own body,
as it kamikazes its own soldiers, it swoops in to end the war.
But remember, Batman ain't without his flaws.
Not everyone is able to be like Ironman.
Medication is to use when needed, not when wanted.
Make a cure to someone's illness legal.

The Ring

Sweat and blood splash off the floor with its warm
presence.
The skin of my back burning and slicing against the
rope,
the bruising, the swelling gets worse around my eyes,
getting hard to see close up like a scope.
A jab makes a clean connection to my face,
the sound of thunder, the shock wave of vibrations
rattling my skull,
sending raindrops of sweat all over the place.
Shot after shot I embrace.
Waiting for a jam or an empty chamber,
a fault in the system I can exploit. I see a path.
I dodge with a swift slight movement, then I unleash my
wrath.
The cracking within my joints,
as I put all of my energy and force into each punch I
land,
cutting and marking his face like a brand.
Chasing him down like wild animal would its prey,
I chisel away as if he was made of stone, making him
unstable, wobbling, no longer able to keep his stature.
I see my opening, quick back hand, like a spark,
lights out, like a torn cable,
flat out like an NBA player.
I launch my gloves up in the air, as if this was a Cold
War,
my adrenaline on come down, my knees hit the floor.
I feel the silky green leather, the golden plate around my
core,
the icy metal pressed against my boiling, bruised skin.
The miles, the pain, the blood and tears, all paid off in
the end.

The Day I Nearly Drowned

Have you ever heard of the saying 'curiosity killed the cat'?
As a kid I must have thought I'd like to put it to the test,
eyeing up the deep end of the pool like it was prey,
as I glide through the shallow end like an alligator.
Until I reach it and suddenly it feels like an anchor is dragging me down.
As I was watched my life bubbling away,
the feet of water stomping on me as if I were the doormat.
Launching my arms out into what felt like the ocean,
my arms became torpedoes, trying to lock onto a target to grip.
I take my last bit of oxygen and start flinging my straw around the cup,
to search for a drop, I missed to sip.
I use my vocals like a cannon ready to explode,
my scream, but it just echoes through the water,
like a recording studio, where it never makes it past the sound proofing.
My arms can't reach out the water no longer,
as if an iceberg was floating above me, my Titanic starts to sink.
My dad's arms have now turned into fishing rods,
he sets his cast and I take the bait.
Without a moment to wait,
I'm hauled through the air,
hitting the ground like a pile of rocks, vomiting out water.
I'm completely disconnected to the computer system of my body,
waiting patiently for it to reboot,
my vocals still on mute.

That was the last time I tried to mess with an instrument;
I don't know how to play like a flute.
I've learnt I just don't float,
you most definitely won't find me on a boat.

Honesty in the Best Policy They Say

My name is Cameron David Simpson.
I'm 6' 3", well I've convinced myself to believe.
I was born 3rd May 2001.
I'm not committed to any religion. I believe that many
different Gods and things are real.

Many of my family have struggled with mental health
through their lives,
and unfortunately, I do too.
I'm in a toxic relationship with fitness,
I've been told I'm too aggressive,
but I tell them I've been fighting my whole life and it's
still not the end of the ride.
No matter how bad it gets, she sticks by my side.

I'm in love with old fashion cars,
I've been told they are at high risk of breaking down,
and to be honest I haven't got a clue how to fix the
problem,
a metaphor for my relationships.

I spend most of my time in a perfect world which I have
built up over the years,
I call it my bedroom.
I have a fear of front doors,
I feel that the world's hand will smash through and
launch me into reality.

I know when you're a kid you have imaginary friends,
I had one.
I have one,
called anger and it's become a little embarrassing,
that it was never imaginary.

I was just playing in front of a mirror.

My worst enemy,
Yes, I said enemy, I know people don't really have
enemies.
But mine is the mirror. No matter how I approach the
battle,
it always exposes my weaknesses.

I box,
I lift weights,
I play video games,
I write poems.
They are the staples that hold my brain together. But
sometimes,
only sometimes,
they are just not strong enough to hold the inevitable.

I have breakdowns.
I'm full of panic.
I watch with a bird's eye view, the nuclear bombs of
anger.
A storm of depression.
A stubborn friend called the past,
that knocks on my door occasionally, to remind me he
still lives here.

One point in my life, I lost control of my tongue,
it moved out of my mouth to marry lies,
then hover around my parents like flies.

So, there is a little bit of honesty.
Honesty which had to be torn out my body like an
organ.
A pleasantly awful experience.

By the way,

I ended up with a new car and it has made me extremely happy.

A TRUE SEND OFF

Promise

I

don't know if it's suicidal,
or not a

promise

I'm

skeptical of the idea of leaving my front door, into a safe
world.

Is it fate that the grim reaper already has a timetable for
when he's

coming

Do I really know I'm coming

home

Is the world only becoming worse?
Will I be catching a ride home in a hearse?

Homicide

Around here a homicide is just another suicide.

This environment is just printing copies out of a stereotypical gangster.

One in a while we evolve.

Fists to blades, then they are broken down to build automatics.
Our tongues no longer dry, and crack under pressure, automatically spraying out "I ain't involved officer, I know my rights officer".

The weapon we keep tucked into our belt.

Today I Was Told I Look Down

"You look really down today, is everything okay?"
Okay.
A word so familiar but so puzzling,
I can never reach further enough into my mind to find
the right answer.
A factory I built purposely to print out my answers,
to be mailed straight to my tongue.
A factory that was originally going with the idea "no",
but the management team said it will use too many
resources and be a waste of time.
The factory went with "I'm fine".
Every day, printing thousands of copies.
Thousands more copies.
I'm fine.
I'm fine.
I'm fine.
I'm fine.
"I'm fine?"
Feeling like I was asking him a rhetorical question.
"Are you sure?"

A Letter from Depression

Dear lover,

I know it's only been a couple of days, but I know deep
down you miss me,
I know you love me.
I know that you have been hiding me,
from your friends,
from your family!
I know you delete our messages,
every time your girlfriend tries taking a sneak peek into
your emotions, which you hold so tightly in your hands.
Someone should tell you that you might want to let them
breathe.
I know you never wanted me to leave.
I've noticed your new poker face you have been wearing,
just know, I can burn that papier-mâché and expose the
storm brewing in your eyes.
I just wanted to say it was fun playing rough last time,
I hope I didn't leave you with too many scars.
I know you weren't feeling too well,
and I could see the happiness crawling up your throat,
trying to throw itself out of your mouth.
So I had trap it shut, leaving you with the burning
sensation like lit cigars,
pressing against the back of your throat, but know I'm
doing what's best for you.
You know you can trust me.
At the end the day, no-one has been by your side longer
than me,
I hope you get this letter,
and I hope you finish that note which you were writing
for me.
I'll be disappointed if you don't.

Acknowledgements

It's common knowledge that to succeed you can plan the execution yourself, to pull it off, that's a whole different challenge in itself. Only with people you trust will you ever get close to even having a glimpse of that dream, to trust your dream might seem the hardest part of the mission. There are those who won't even think to sabotage your vision but will help you to accomplish what you set out to build on the foundation you started to place.

On that note:

Thank you to my parents for pushing me in the direction of the path I've always tried to take but had temporarily strayed away from.

Thank you to my grandparents for encouraging me to take the small idea which I'd pushed to the side, which has now expanded to larger than I could ever have hoped.

Thank you to my friends for the honest, not too mean, feedback and for putting me back on track when I derailed.

Thank you to the family member who helped to chisel the art which I wanted the rock of my foundation to look like.

Thank you to those who didn't shy away from offering me a helping hand through those stand-still points during the process.

Thank you to my siblings for their knowledge, honest feedback and support.

Thank you to the one who is always by my side and pushes me to be the best I can, who won't let me have doubt in my head and keeps me standing tall.

Simply I'm thankful to have all these people in my life.

About the Author

Cameron Simpson is an English poet and music creator who uses poetry and lyrics to portray topics close to his heart such as mental health, family values and the effects of crime. His references to mythology and pop culture provide an opening to these serious subjects.